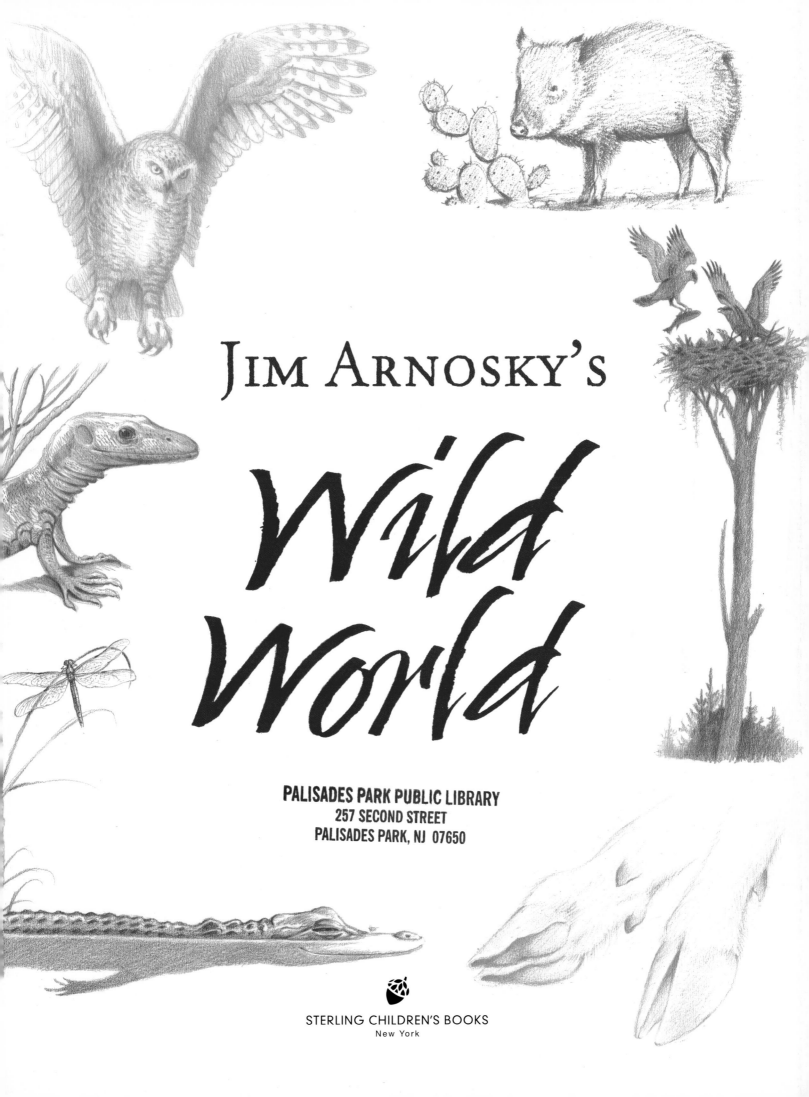

Jim Arnosky's
Wild World

STERLING CHILDREN'S BOOKS
New York

STERLING CHILDREN'S BOOKS
New York

An Imprint of Sterling Publishing
387 Park Avenue South
New York, NY 10016

Wild Tracks originally published in 2008 by Sterling Publishing
Slither and Crawl originally published in 2009 by Sterling Publishing
Thunder Birds originally published in 2011 by Sterling Publishing

Text © 2008, 2009, 2011, 2014 by Jim Arnosky
Illustrations © 2008, 2009, 2011, 2014 by Jim Arnosky
The artwork for this book was created using pencil and acrylic paints.

ISBN 978-1-4549-1344-3

Distributed in Canada by Sterling Publishing
c/o Canadian Manda Group, 165 Dufferin Street
Toronto, Ontario, Canada M6K 3H6
Distributed in the United Kingdom by GMC Distribution Services
Castle Place, 166 High Street, Lewes, East Sussex, England BN7 1XU
Distributed in Australia by Capricorn Link (Australia) Pty. Ltd.
P.O. Box 704, Windsor, NSW 2756, Australia

Designed by Andrea Miller, Merideth Harte, Lauren Rille

For information about custom editions, special sales, and premium and corporate purchases, please contact Sterling Special Sales at 800-805-5489 or specialsales@sterlingpublishing.com.

Manufactured in China
Lot #:
10 9 8 7 6 5 4 3 2 1
06/14

www.sterlingpublishing.com/kids

CONTENTS

THUNDER BIRDS: Nature's Flying Predators

ADDITIONAL READING

Preface

The marks and tracks an animal leaves behind are a written record that can be read if you learn the language. The first part of this book, "Wild Tracks," will teach you how to decipher animal tracks. Included are life-size tracks of 84 mammals, birds, and reptiles, as well as many other identifying marks animals make on trees and in sand and snow.

Reptiles slither. Reptiles crawl. Reptiles are the most fascinating creatures of all! Find out for yourself in the second section of this book, "Slither and Crawl." When I first set out to study reptiles, I did so reluctantly. My lifelong fear of snakes dampened my spirit. Fortunately, my wife, Deanna, who has no fear of snakes or any other reptiles, found for me all I needed to write about and paint. And as I learned about each species with her, I began to see them as she sees them—beautiful and interesting. I began to seek out reptiles with renewed enthusiasm, admiration, and wonder.

"Thunder Birds" is a name I have given to our largest and most formidable birds—as you will see in the third section of this book. Birds that hunt. Birds that fish. Big birds that command our attention as they soar high in the sky or dive into the waves. Plunge into this section of the book with your eyes wide open to see the close-up details that make nature's flying predators so colorful and fascinating.

This book explores three very diverse wildlife groups. With its fourteen spectacular fold-out pages, it is a wide open, friendly, and inviting gateway to the wild. Enjoy!

Jim Arnosky

ANHINGA

WILD TRACKS!

A GUIDE TO NATURE'S FOOTPRINTS

When you learn to recognize and read animal tracks you are learning an ancient language of shapes and patterns. The shapes of the footprints reveal the identity of the track maker. The pattern of the tracks tells a story about what the animal was doing. In the painting on the opposite page, the large web-footed tracks, deeply pressed in the sand, show that a waterbird (in this case an anhinga) was fishing underwater and swam to shore. It walked water-logged and heavily for a few steps and hopped up onto a branch to dry off or swallow a fish or both.

I have been studying animal tracks ever since I was a boy and became curious about the wildlife living around my home. My wildlife journals are filled with sketches of tracks and track patterns that show various animals walking, running, or leaping.

On the pages that follow, I will show you animals making tracks in their natural habitats and dozens of wild animal footprints, many of which I have painted life-size.

So start making tracks of your own outdoors! Look around. See what animals live near you, and learn to read the stories their tracks tell.

WHITE-TAILED DEER

Deer Tracks

The heart-shaped hoofprints of deer are the most recognizable of all animal tracks. Male deer tend to drag their feet as they walk. The bigger the buck, the deeper the drag marks.

When deer run, their sharp hoofs cut deeply into the ground and their small back toes, called dewclaws, can often be seen in their tracks. Deer running or walking on slippery mud or ice spread their hoofs wide for stability, making their hoofprints look like a set of horns. Reverse hoofprints indicate the deer made an abrupt turnabout to run away. In autumn—the deer's breeding season—look for fresh marks on small trees where bark has been worn away. These "buck rubs" are made by the antlers of male deer while they are practicing to fight with other males.

The white-tailed deer, shown on the left, is typical of the North American deer family, which also includes elk, caribou, and moose.

Buck drags in light snow

An abrupt turnabout

4½'

Deer walking

Deer running

Buck rubs

Bottom of a deer hoof

Toenails

Toes

Dewclaw

Top of a deer hoof

AMERICAN BUFFALO

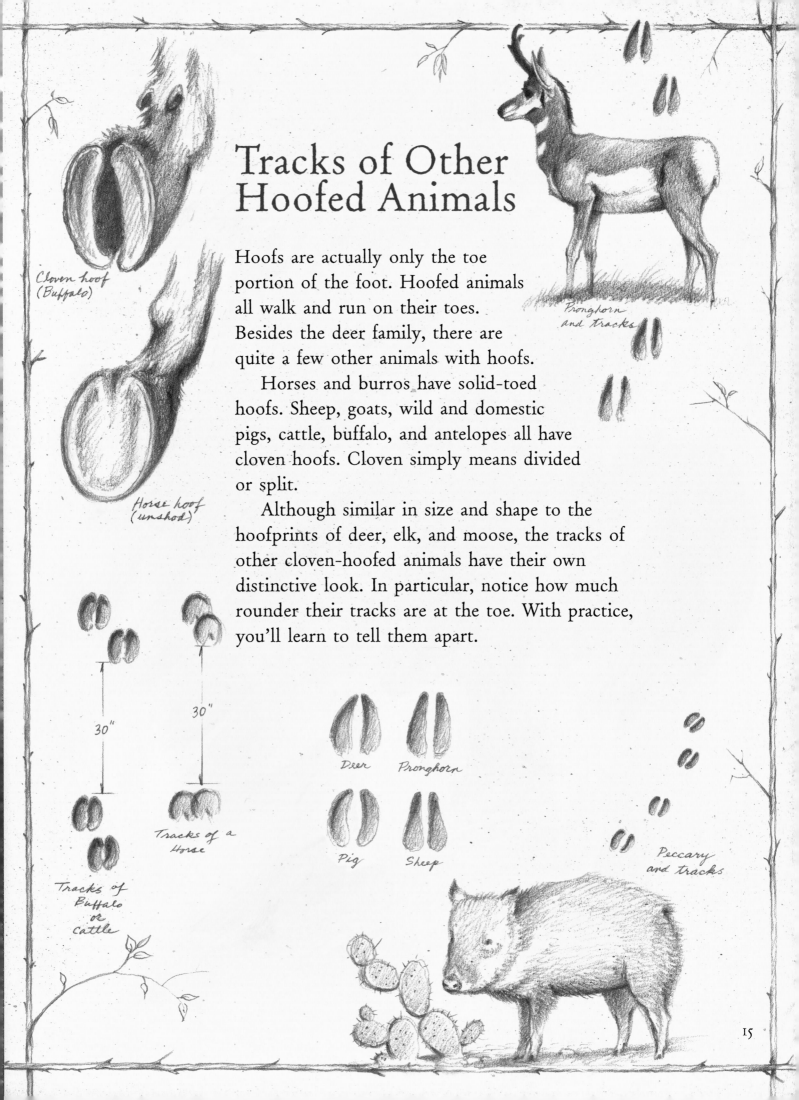

Tracks of Other Hoofed Animals

Hoofs are actually only the toe portion of the foot. Hoofed animals all walk and run on their toes. Besides the deer family, there are quite a few other animals with hoofs.

Horses and burros have solid-toed hoofs. Sheep, goats, wild and domestic pigs, cattle, buffalo, and antelopes all have cloven hoofs. Cloven simply means divided or split.

Although similar in size and shape to the hoofprints of deer, elk, and moose, the tracks of other cloven-hoofed animals have their own distinctive look. In particular, notice how much rounder their tracks are at the toe. With practice, you'll learn to tell them apart.

Cloven hoof
(Buffalo)

Horse hoof
(unshod)

Pronghorn
and tracks

30"

30"

Tracks of a
Horse

Tracks of
Buffalo
or
cattle

Deer   Pronghorn

Pig   Sheep

Peccary
and tracks

15

BLACK BEAR

Bear Tracks

Bears walk flatfooted, placing the entire foot on the ground with each step. The wide front feet and the large hind feet show completely in bear tracks. When running, the front feet and the front portion of the hind feet show up in the tracks. Because a bear is a heavy animal, its tracks are often pressed deeply, creating perfectly defined footprints. With a perfect set of four bear footprints (two front and two hind), an experienced animal tracker is able to accurately estimate the size and weight of the bear that made them.

On slippery surfaces, a bear's toes spread apart for better traction, pressing in footprints that are much larger than the bear's feet. Such splayed footprints can fool a tracker into imagining the bear that left them is much larger than its actual size.

Black Bear tracks in soft ground

A splayed Track

Running fast

A Track pattern of a Black Bear running slowly

4'

4'

Black Bear claw marks on tree

Bottom of a Black Bear's hind foot

Black Bear Claw (actual size)

Bottom of a Black Bear's front foot

LIFE-SIZE TRACKS OF BEARS

BLACK BEAR
The black bear is found throughout North America. It is the smallest of the North American bears, which include the grizzly, brown, and polar bears.

GRIZZLY BEAR and BROWN BEAR
(note marks of long claws)

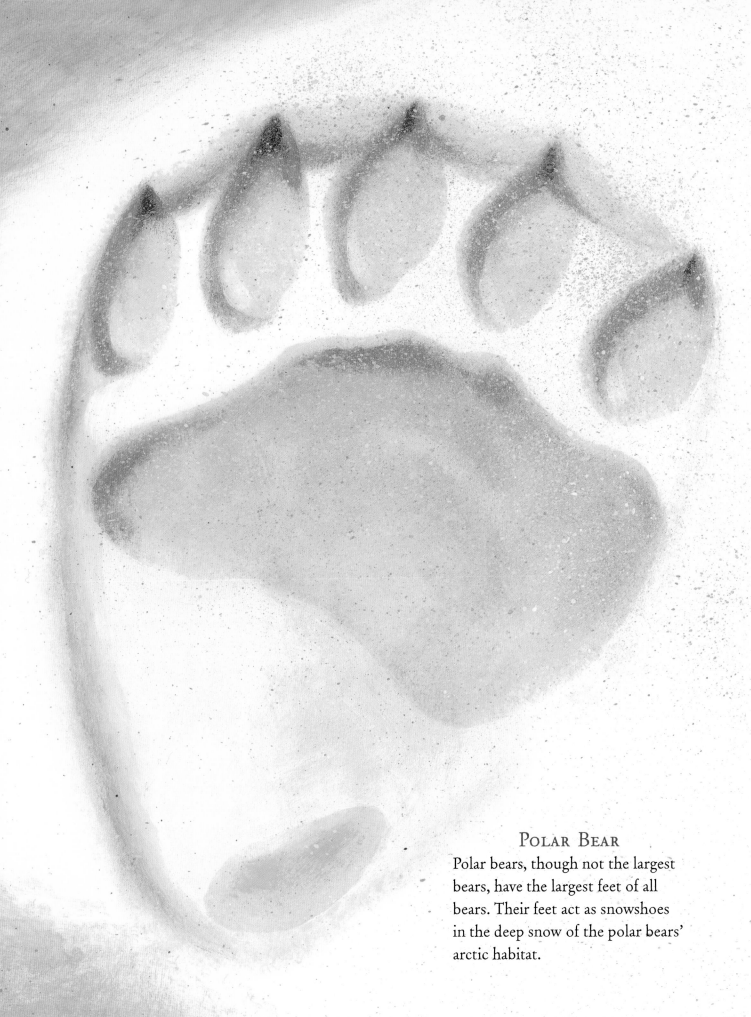

POLAR BEAR

Polar bears, though not the largest
bears, have the largest feet of all
bears. Their feet act as snowshoes
in the deep snow of the polar bears'
arctic habitat.

SNOWSHOE HARE

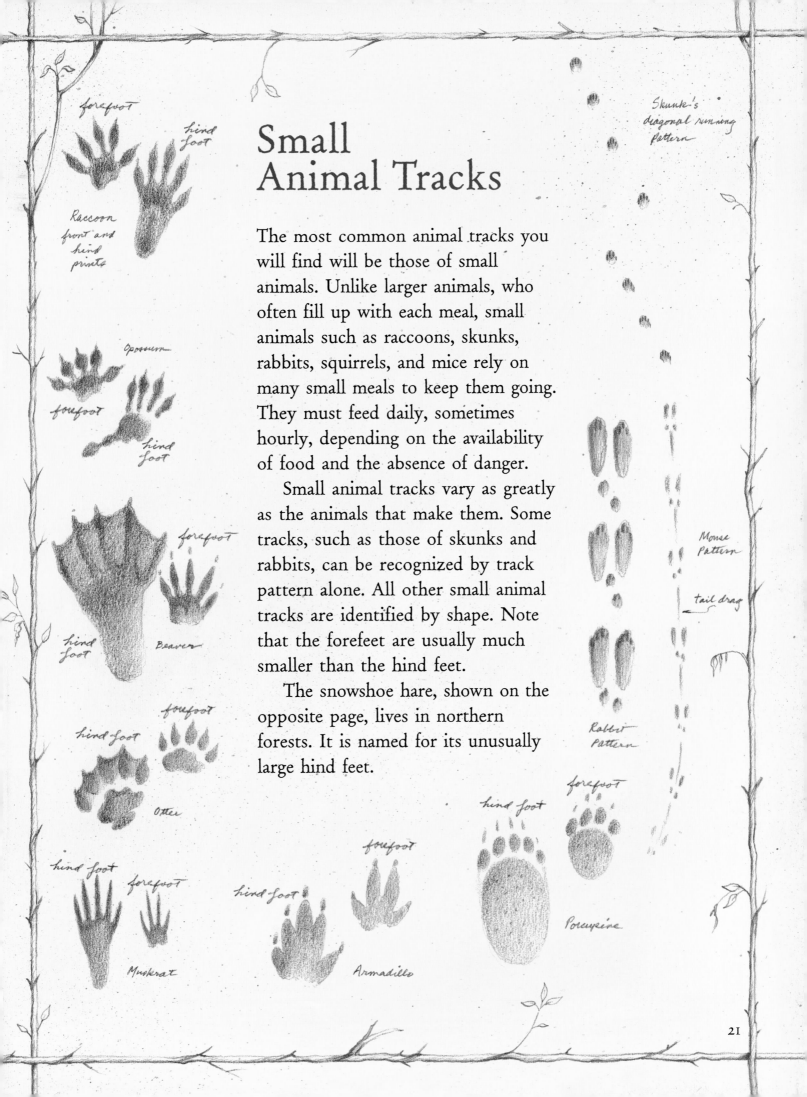

Small Animal Tracks

The most common animal tracks you will find will be those of small animals. Unlike larger animals, who often fill up with each meal, small animals such as raccoons, skunks, rabbits, squirrels, and mice rely on many small meals to keep them going. They must feed daily, sometimes hourly, depending on the availability of food and the absence of danger.

Small animal tracks vary as greatly as the animals that make them. Some tracks, such as those of skunks and rabbits, can be recognized by track pattern alone. All other small animal tracks are identified by shape. Note that the forefeet are usually much smaller than the hind feet.

The snowshoe hare, shown on the opposite page, lives in northern forests. It is named for its unusually large hind feet.

forefoot

hind foot

Raccoon front and hind prints

Opossum

forefoot

hind foot

forefoot

hind foot

Beaver

forefoot

hind foot

Otter

hind foot

forefoot

Muskrat

hind foot

forefoot

Armadillo

hind foot

forefoot

Porcupine

Skunk's diagonal running pattern

Mouse Pattern

tail drag

Rabbit Pattern

LIFE-SIZE TRACKS
OF SMALL ANIMALS

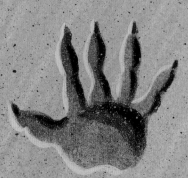

RACCOON
forefoot

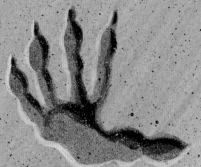

OPOSSUM
hind foot

MINK
forefoot

**LONG-TAILED
WEASEL**
forefoot

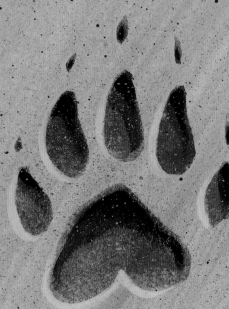

BADGER
forefoot

STRIPED SKUNK
forefoot

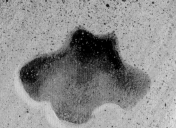

RIVER OTTER
hind foot

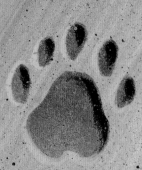

RINGTAIL
forefoot

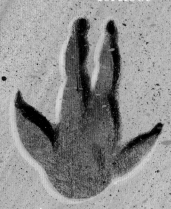

ARMADILLO
forefoot

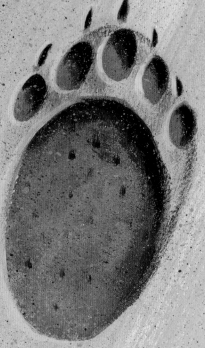

PORCUPINE
hind foot

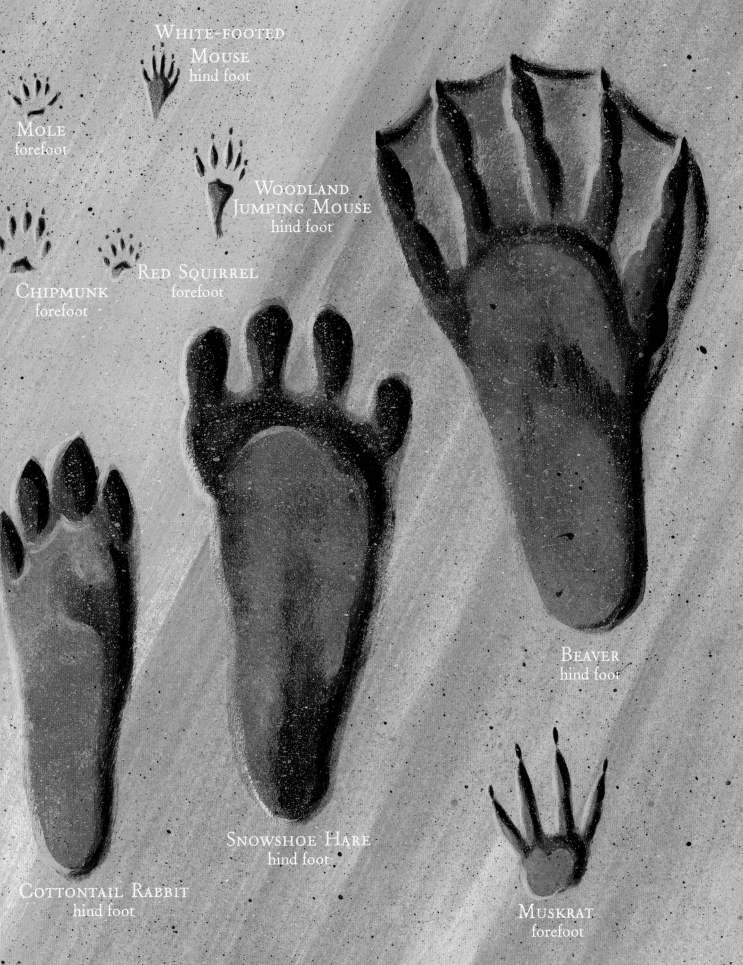

White-footed Mouse
hind foot

Mole
forefoot

Woodland
Jumping Mouse
hind foot

Chipmunk
forefoot

Red Squirrel
forefoot

Beaver
hind foot

Cottontail Rabbit
hind foot

Snowshoe Hare
hind foot

Muskrat
forefoot

23

BOBCAT

Feline Tracks

Of all the larger predators, wildcats are the most likely to use the same trails again and again. In deep snow, their habitual routes become gully trails in which feline tracks going to and coming from their hunting grounds are preserved, down out of the wind, away from blowing snow.

A cat's sharp retractable claws do not show in its tracks unless the cat has lunged to catch its prey or scratched the ground to cover its droppings. Only cats thoroughly cover their droppings.

Bobcat, lion, and jaguar paws all have three-lobed heels. The lynx, the ocelot, and the jaguarundi have single-lobed heels.

The wildcats we have in North America are, from smallest to largest: ocelot, jaguarundi, bobcat, lynx, American lion, and jaguar.

Typical cat print

Lynx

20" Domestic cat

36" Bobcat

Cat walking

Note claw marks

Cat running and lunging after prey

Tracks poked in deep snow

Bobcat foot - top
showing retractable claws

Bottom
showing 3-lobed heel

TIMBER WOLF

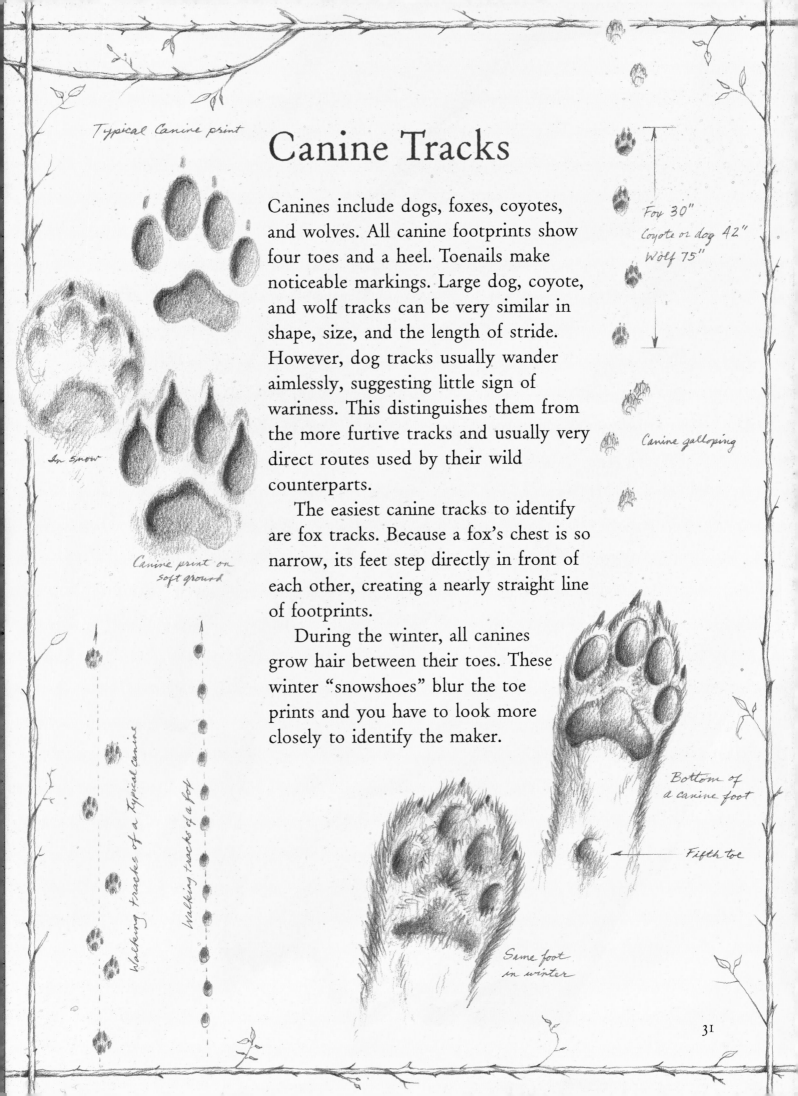

Canine Tracks

Canines include dogs, foxes, coyotes, and wolves. All canine footprints show four toes and a heel. Toenails make noticeable markings. Large dog, coyote, and wolf tracks can be very similar in shape, size, and the length of stride. However, dog tracks usually wander aimlessly, suggesting little sign of wariness. This distinguishes them from the more furtive tracks and usually very direct routes used by their wild counterparts.

The easiest canine tracks to identify are fox tracks. Because a fox's chest is so narrow, its feet step directly in front of each other, creating a nearly straight line of footprints.

During the winter, all canines grow hair between their toes. These winter "snowshoes" blur the toe prints and you have to look more closely to identify the maker.

Typical canine print

In snow

Canine print on soft ground

Walking tracks of a Typical Canine

Walking tracks of a fox

Fox 30"
Coyote or dog 42"
Wolf 75"

Canine galloping

Bottom of a canine foot

Fifth toe

Same foot in winter

COTTONMOUTH MOCCASIN
AND WHITE IBISES

Reptile & Bird Tracks

Reptile tracks often go unnoticed. Our eyes are used to looking for distinctive footprints rather than the various scrapes and marks reptiles make. But when a snake slithers across mud or a turtle drags itself over sand, a series of tracks are left that are very recognizable.

During times of drought, alligator tracks can be seen on the mud flats that were previously covered by water. Use only your binoculars to examine reptile tracks. Never follow on foot. The places where these animals go can be unsafe, and the animals can be dangerous if approached suddenly.

Bird tracks rarely travel far before their makers take flight. Some bird tracks show only two footprints and the wing marks as the bird flaps away. Songbirds hop. Shorebirds and large birds such as crows, geese, and turkeys walk. All birds create the most delicate and beautiful animal tracks, evoking both earth and sky in every footprint.

Snake tracks

Alligator tracks

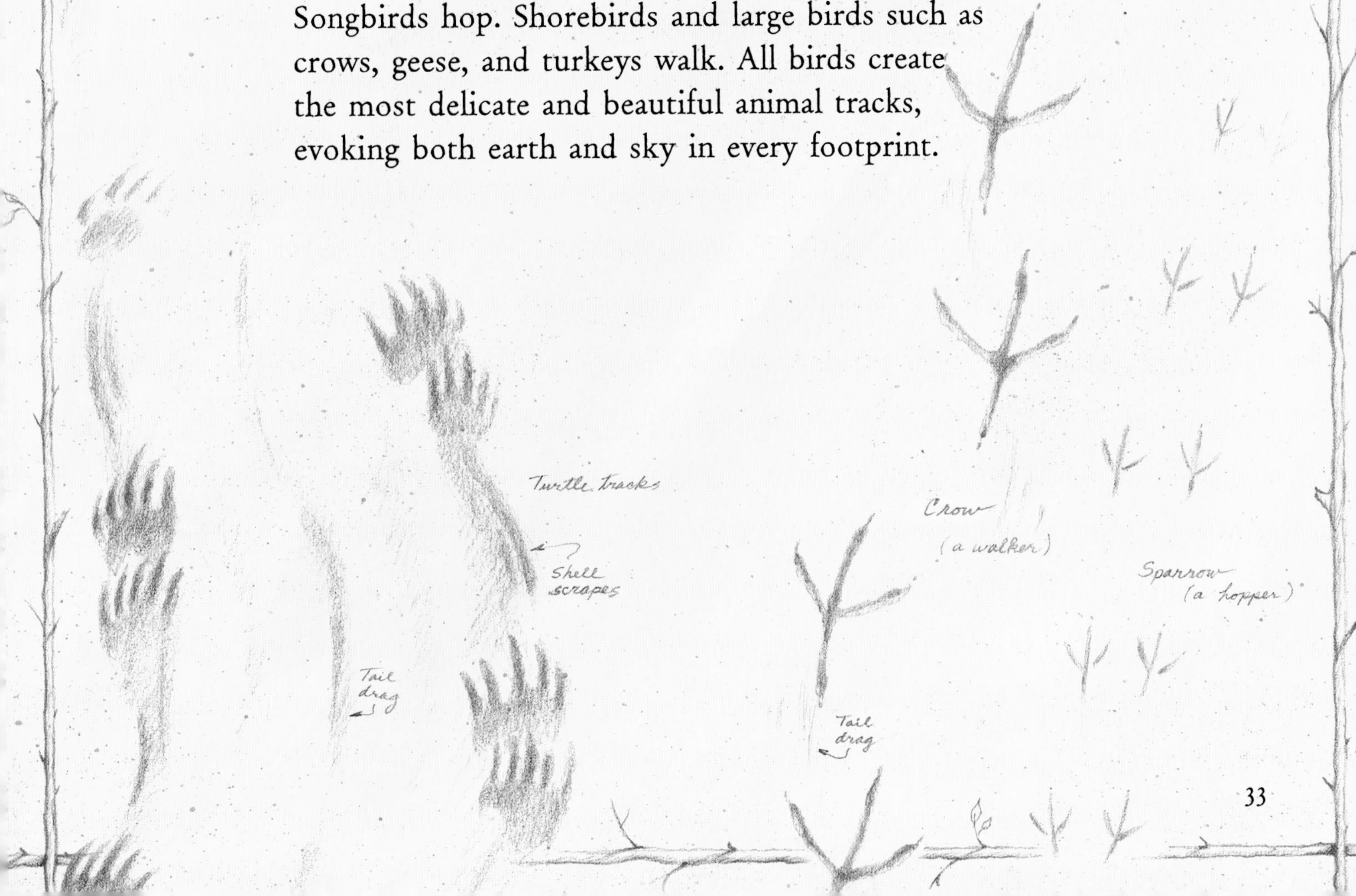

Turtle tracks

Shell scrapes

Tail drag

Tail drag

Crow
(a walker)

Sparrow
(a hopper)

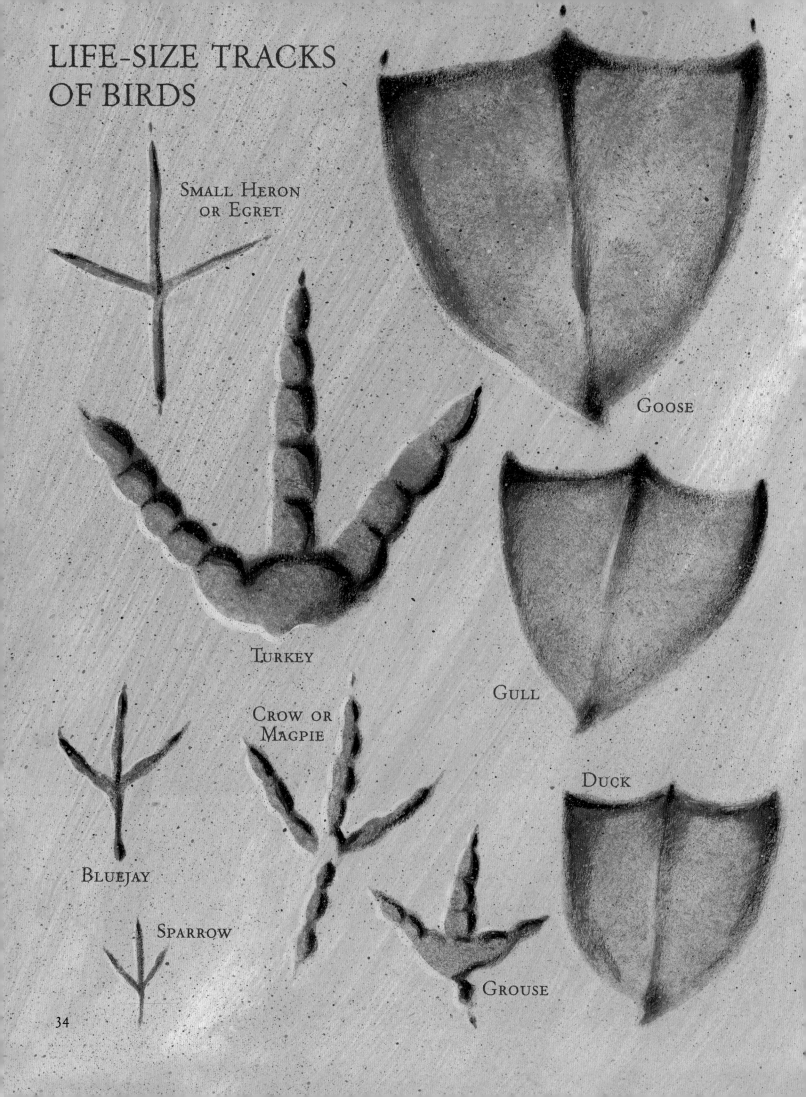

LIFE-SIZE TRACKS OF BIRDS

SMALL HERON OR EGRET

TURKEY

BLUEJAY

CROW OR MAGPIE

SPARROW

GROUSE

GOOSE

GULL

DUCK

34

AUTHOR'S NOTE

The deer walked briskly along the snowy trail, stepping over fallen branches and around tree trunks until it came to a steep knoll. With its hooves digging into the earth beneath the snow, it crossed the knoll in two bounds and continued hurriedly along the high hill spine. Something had frightened or was pursuing it, making the deer walk very quickly, kicking up snow and wet brown leaves. When it came to a well-worn deer path that led steeply downhill, the deer began to run. Faster and faster it coursed down the slanting trail, leaping over small evergreens, keeping balance by splaying its hooves wide, skidding and sliding but never falling. It was a story written clearly in the snow—a story I read today in the deer's tracks left in the woods behind my house in Vermont.

All forms of writing are marks made on a surface. Pictures, as well as words, evoke images and stories in our minds. Similarly, every animal track reveals something about the animal that made it, and a set or series of tracks records a small part of the story of where it went and what it was doing.

Animal tracks on soft ground last. You can revisit them again and again before they fade, are washed away by rain, or become overprinted by fresher footprints.

Animal tracks in snow rarely last long. Each new snowfall covers them and lays down a new, white page on which other tracks will be made.

The next time you go outdoors, look for wild tracks. There may be a fascinating story at your feet, imprinted in the mud or snow or scratched into the sand. You needn't go far to learn something interesting about the wild track makers. And when you go home, you will be leaving a little part of the story of your day in the footprints *you* have made.

ALLIGATOR

Loggerhead
sea turtle

SLITHER and CRAWL

EYE TO EYE WITH REPTILES

Growing up in Pennsylvania, I dreamed of wild places where snakes slithered across jungle trails, lizards climbed on twisted branches of trees, and alligators crawled out of the water onto lush green banks. Reptiles have always captured my imagination in a way no other animals do.

Reptiles are cold-blooded. They cannot warm themselves internally the way birds and mammals can. Reptiles find sun to warm up and shade to cool down.

Reptiles include turtles, snakes, lizards, and crocodilians. In the United States, there are many different species of turtles, snakes, and lizards, but only two native crocodilians: crocodiles and alligators. Most of the reptiles in this book are native to North America. A few are native to other parts of the world. I have included them to give you an idea of just how broad a variety of reptiles there are.

Many reptiles are harmless. Just as many are dangerous. Some are venomous (poisonous). When I'm watching dangerous reptiles in the wild, I use binoculars or a telephoto camera lens so that I can see them clearly, but from a safe distance. You can get a close-up view of all the reptiles in this book just by looking at my life-size paintings. So belly down on the ground, eye to reptilian eye, and read all about these fascinating animals that slither and crawl.

Chuckwalla lizard

Yellow-Rat Snake

37

BANDED WATER SNAKE

Snakes

I was crawling on my elbows toward an amber-colored trout pool. Suddenly, right in front of me, a banded water snake looped down from the lowest branch of a streamside tree. For a moment we were eye to eye. Then the snake dropped to the ground and slithered into the water.

Snakes are reptiles that have no limbs (legs). Snakes have scaly skin and jaws that unhinge to open wide and swallow prey whole. Snakes have no eyelids, but transparent skin protects the snake's eyes. Broad grasping belly scales enable snakes to crawl and climb. Belly, back, and head scales waterproof the snake's body and prevent it from losing the moisture it needs. The scales on a snake's back are either smooth or keeled, depending on the species. Keeled scales have a ridge down the center, like the keel on the bottom of a boat.

There are more than 2,500 species of snakes in the world. While most begin life in the egg, many species are born live from the mother. As a snake grows, it periodically sheds its skin. The old skin, dry and dull in color, loosens and peels off in one piece, giving way to more supple, brilliantly colored new skin.

A wide triangular head usually means a snake is venomous. The triangular shape allows space for a venom sac above each jaw. Venom from such sacs is injected into prey through hollow fangs when the snake bites. Not all species of venomous snakes have triangular heads. Coral snakes and cobras, for example, are venomous but have oval heads.

Rattlesnake warning "Go away!"

Rattlesnake skull showing hollow fangs. Fangs hinge back against roof of mouth when not biting.

Hognose snake spreading neck skin to feign ferocity

Triangular head

Oval head

41

BROWN ANOLE

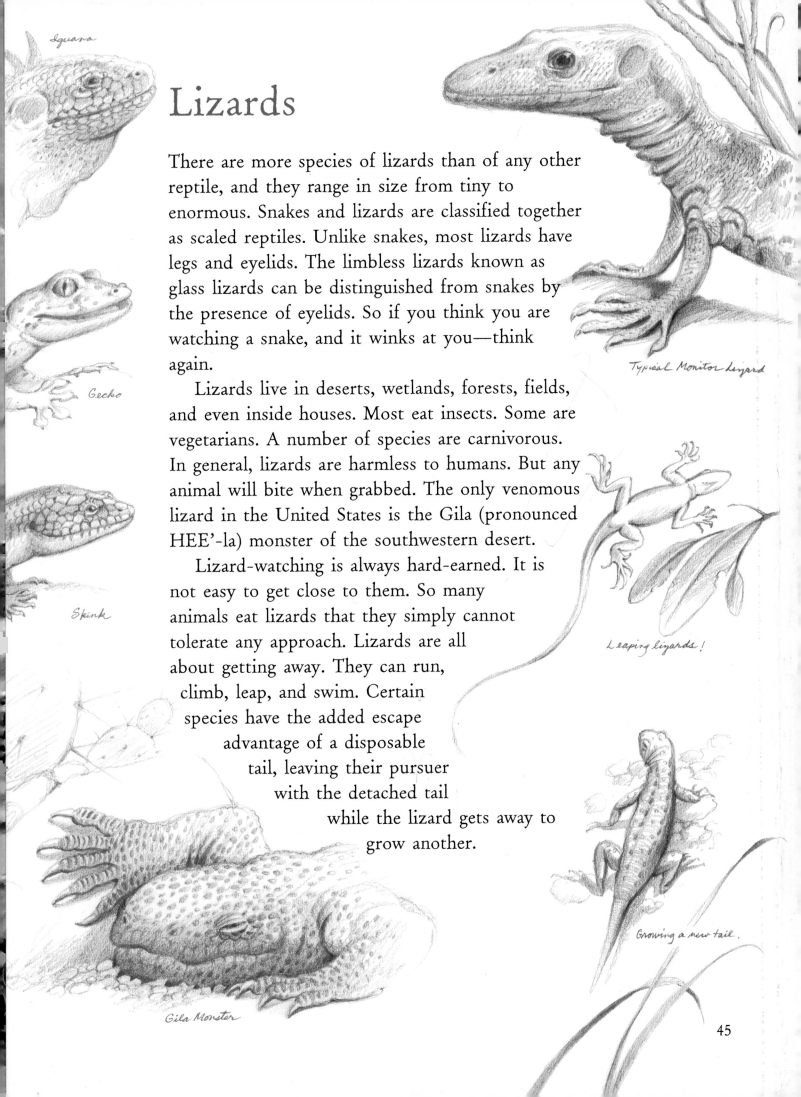

Lizards

There are more species of lizards than of any other reptile, and they range in size from tiny to enormous. Snakes and lizards are classified together as scaled reptiles. Unlike snakes, most lizards have legs and eyelids. The limbless lizards known as glass lizards can be distinguished from snakes by the presence of eyelids. So if you think you are watching a snake, and it winks at you—think again.

Lizards live in deserts, wetlands, forests, fields, and even inside houses. Most eat insects. Some are vegetarians. A number of species are carnivorous. In general, lizards are harmless to humans. But any animal will bite when grabbed. The only venomous lizard in the United States is the Gila (pronounced HEE'-la) monster of the southwestern desert.

Lizard-watching is always hard-earned. It is not easy to get close to them. So many animals eat lizards that they simply cannot tolerate any approach. Lizards are all about getting away. They can run, climb, leap, and swim. Certain species have the added escape advantage of a disposable tail, leaving their pursuer with the detached tail while the lizard gets away to grow another.

Iguana

Gecko

Skink

Typical Monitor Lizard

Leaping lizards!

Growing a new tail.

Gila Monster

45

KOMODO DRAGON
(INDONESIA)

GIGANTIC LIZARDS

Some lizard species grow to gigantic sizes. Green iguanas and rhinoceros iguanas can grow to be 5 feet long or more. The largest lizards in the world are the monitor lizards, and the largest monitor lizard is the Komodo dragon of Indonesia. These giants grow to be 10 feet long, stand 2 feet tall at the shoulder, and weigh over 200 pounds.

RHINOCEROS IGUANA
(DOMINICAN REPUBLIC)
Rhinoceros iguanas are named for the hornlike bump on their foreheads.

GARTER SNAKES

Where Do Reptiles
Go in Winter?

Though snakes, alligators, and crocodiles occasionally migrate to find water or better hunting areas, they, and many other reptiles, are not made for any long-distance seasonal migration. Unlike birds that can leave cold weather and fly hundreds, even thousands of miles to warmer places, reptiles have to stay put and endure the cold.

All reptiles react to cold weather by becoming sluggish and inactive. They find a place out of the wind and lie low. Crocodiles and alligators submerge most of their bodies in warm water or wallow in mud. Lizards retreat to available holes or crevices or simply cling to the innermost branches of trees. Turtles that live in water find warmer water. Land turtles dig in, retreat inside their shells, and tough out cold spells.

In places where winter is cold for months at a time, reptiles hibernate in mud or leaf litter. Some species hibernate communally, in rocky crevices or dens. Every winter garter snakes congregate to hibernate in a den under our house's stone foundation. It doesn't really feel like spring around our place until the snakes emerge, often all at once!

Alligator in
muddy water.

GIANT TORTOISE

Turtles

Tough and durable, turtles have been around since the dawn of the dinosaurs. There are 250 species of turtles living today.

Turtles are reptiles with protective shells made of strong bone—a top shell (carapace) and a bottom shell (plastron). Some turtles can hide completely inside their shells. The box turtle's hinged plastron clamps closed like a vacuum-sealed lid when the turtle pulls inside. Turtles that can only partially hide inside their shells have large front legs that block and protect their partially exposed heads.

There are land turtles and water turtles. Many species of land turtles have extra-tough skin and thick scales on their legs to protect them from bruises they might get when clambering over rugged terrain.

Tortoises are the largest land turtles. In dry country, they dig burrows in the sand. Besides providing protection from cuts and scratches while digging, a tortoise's thick skin helps to keep the tortoise from drying out.

Land turtles eat vegetation and insects. Swift and agile water turtles catch and eat fish. Big snapping turtles eat fish, swimming birds, and rodents.

Carapace

Plastron

Box Turtle

Gopher Tortoise

Snapping Turtle

Snapping Turtle

Turtles have keen eyesight.

Hinge

Box Turtle's hinged bottom shell clamped closed. Turtle inside.

Sea Turtle

Some turtles can be identified by shape alone.

Softshell Turtle

51

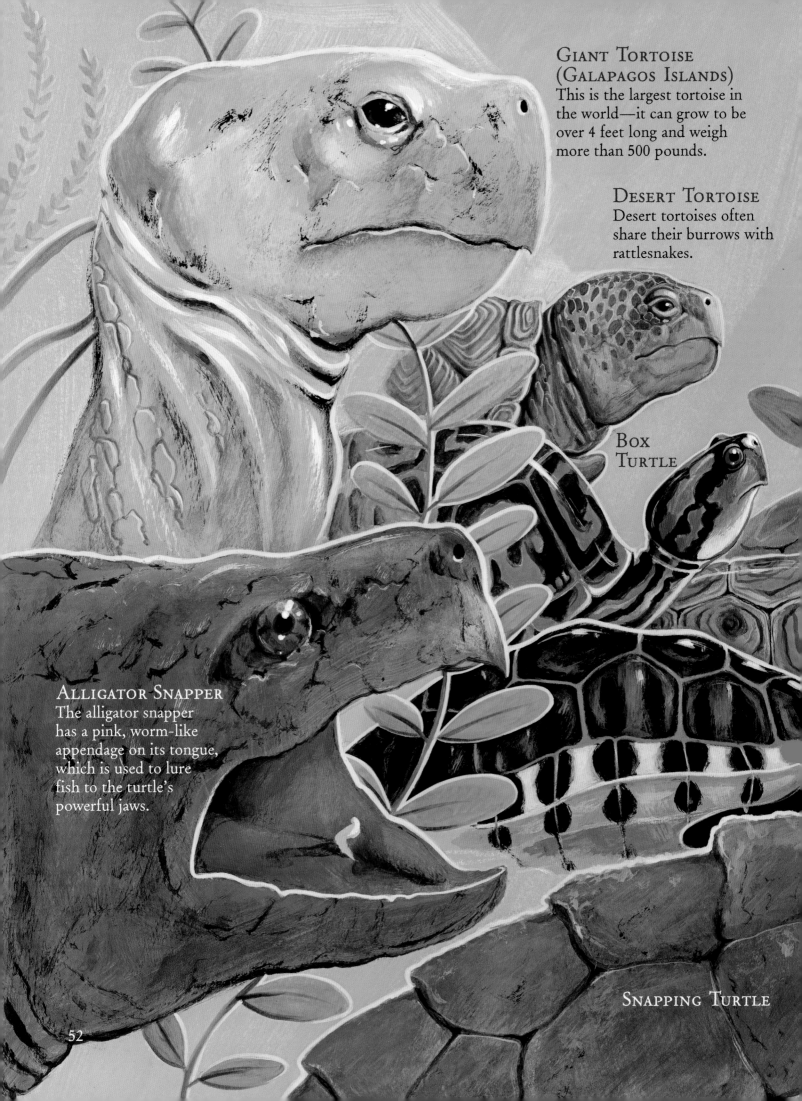

GIANT TORTOISE (GALAPAGOS ISLANDS)
This is the largest tortoise in the world—it can grow to be over 4 feet long and weigh more than 500 pounds.

DESERT TORTOISE
Desert tortoises often share their burrows with rattlesnakes.

BOX TURTLE

ALLIGATOR SNAPPER
The alligator snapper has a pink, worm-like appendage on its tongue, which is used to lure fish to the turtle's powerful jaws.

SNAPPING TURTLE

52

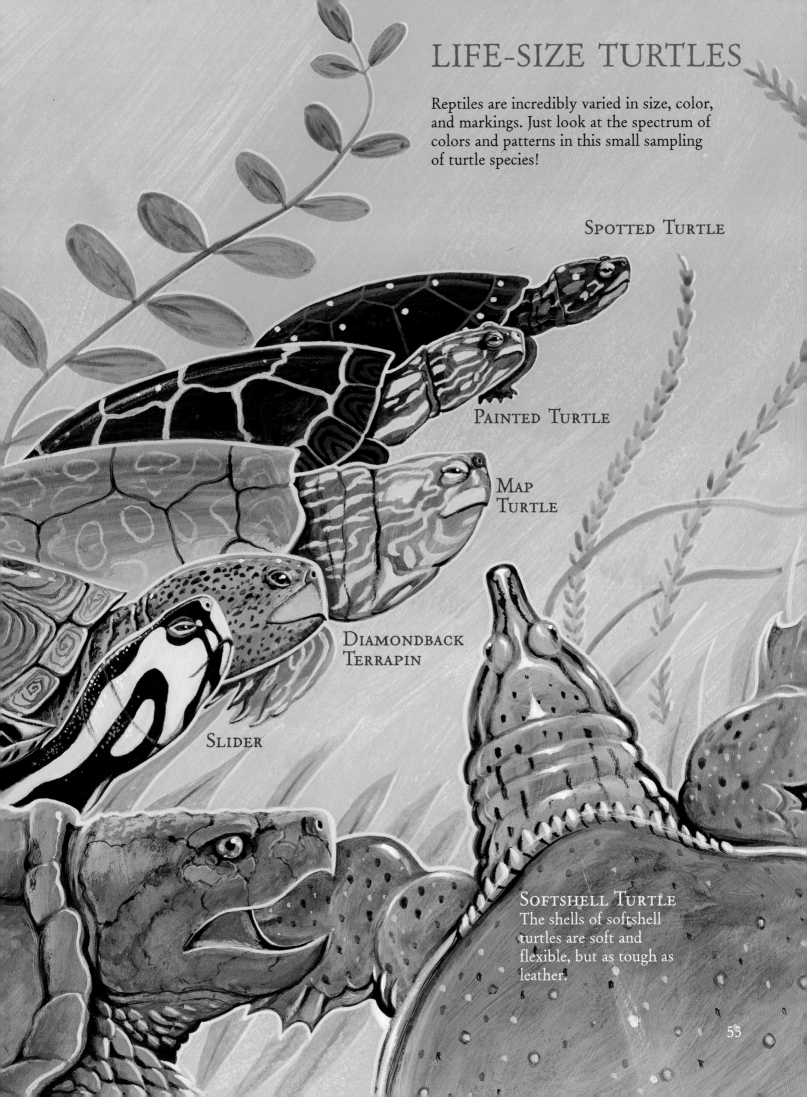

LIFE-SIZE TURTLES

Reptiles are incredibly varied in size, color, and markings. Just look at the spectrum of colors and patterns in this small sampling of turtle species!

SPOTTED TURTLE

PAINTED TURTLE

MAP TURTLE

DIAMONDBACK TERRAPIN

SLIDER

SOFTSHELL TURTLE
The shells of softshell turtles are soft and flexible, but as tough as leather.

LOGGERHEAD SEA TURTLE AND PORK FISH

Sea Turtles

In the warm and shallow waters of Florida Bay, I often see sea turtles—mostly loggerheads—splashing after floating jellyfish. The turtles seem to be curious about the world around them. Once in a while, one will surface near my boat and look me over before diving back under.

Sea turtles are completely aquatic. They do not crawl out of the water to sun themselves the way freshwater turtles do.

Female sea turtles come on land only to lay and bury their eggs. They crawl onshore, dragging their heavy bodies on the sand. It is an arduous task. The weightlessness they feel in water is suddenly gone. Once they deposit their eggs, they abandon them and return to the sea. In all species of turtles, hatchlings fend for themselves. After baby sea turtles have dug themselves out of the nest, they rush to the relative safety of the sea. The males never again return to land.

As light and agile in the water as they are heavy and cumbersome on land, sea turtles feed on fish, crabs, mollusks, seaweed, algae, sponges, and jellyfish.

All sea turtles, except for the leatherback, have plated shells similar to the shells of land and freshwater turtles. The leatherback's leathery carapace is ridged, not plated.

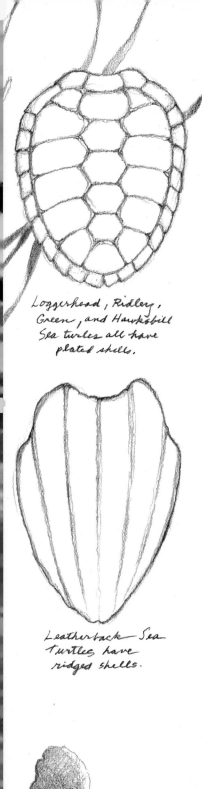

Loggerhead, Ridley, Green, and Hawksbill Sea turtles all have plated shells.

Leatherback Sea Turtles have ridged shells.

Baby Sea turtles in the sea.

The Leatherback's main diet consists of jellyfish!

Leatherbacks grow to be eight feet long overall, and weigh 1000 to 1200 pounds.

AMERICAN CROCODILE

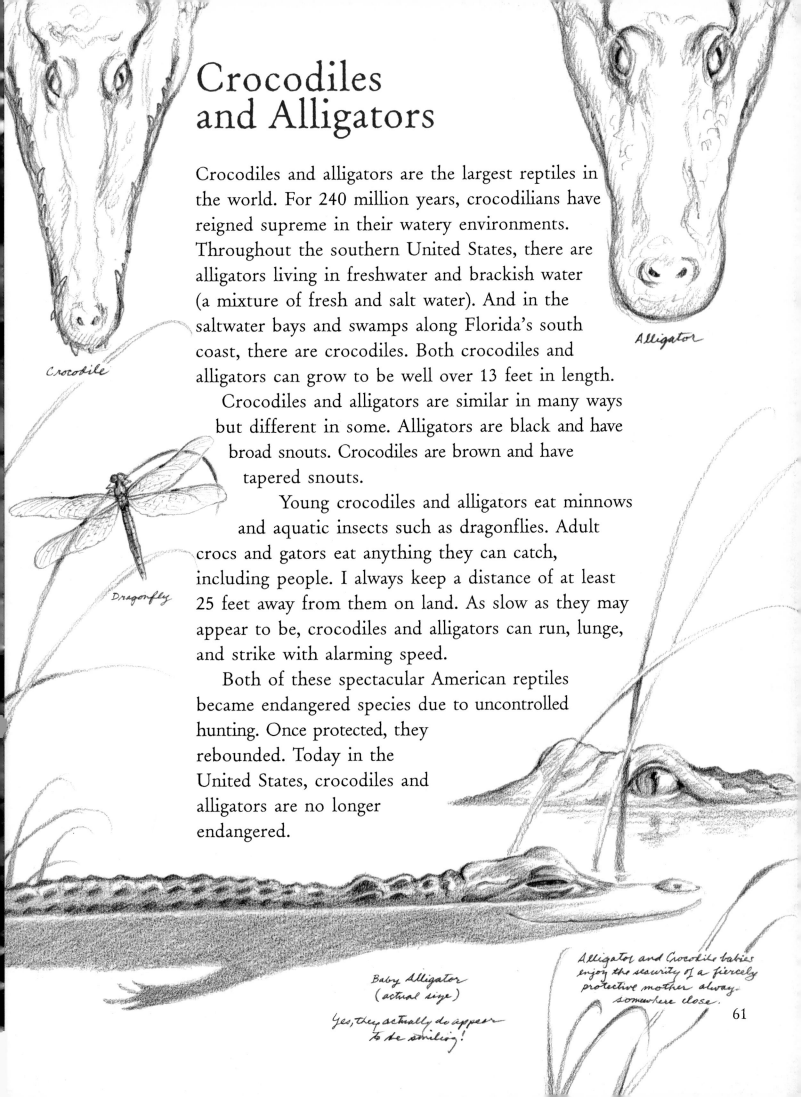

Crocodiles and Alligators

Crocodiles and alligators are the largest reptiles in the world. For 240 million years, crocodilians have reigned supreme in their watery environments. Throughout the southern United States, there are alligators living in freshwater and brackish water (a mixture of fresh and salt water). And in the saltwater bays and swamps along Florida's south coast, there are crocodiles. Both crocodiles and alligators can grow to be well over 13 feet in length.

Crocodiles and alligators are similar in many ways but different in some. Alligators are black and have broad snouts. Crocodiles are brown and have tapered snouts.

Young crocodiles and alligators eat minnows and aquatic insects such as dragonflies. Adult crocs and gators eat anything they can catch, including people. I always keep a distance of at least 25 feet away from them on land. As slow as they may appear to be, crocodiles and alligators can run, lunge, and strike with alarming speed.

Both of these spectacular American reptiles became endangered species due to uncontrolled hunting. Once protected, they rebounded. Today in the United States, crocodiles and alligators are no longer endangered.

Crocodile

Alligator

Dragonfly

Baby Alligator
(actual size)
Yes, they actually do appear
to be smiling!

Alligator and Crocodile babies
enjoy the security of a fiercely
protective mother always
somewhere close.

61

BURMESE PYTHON

A Richness of Reptiles

There are well over 6,000 species of reptiles in the world, living in the oceans and on all continents except Antarctica. The world is rich with reptiles. Their presence fills any outing with a sense of excitement. At any moment, something very much alive and wild may slither or crawl by your feet, sending shivers up your spine.

Recently, while hiking through a tropical hardwood forest in Key Largo, Florida, I felt that excitement in a big way. I was looking for snakes—in particular, one of the pythons reported to be living there. Pythons are large constrictors closely related to boas. Although they are not native to the United States, pythons descended from illegally released pets have been breeding and thriving in the Florida Everglades for years. Now they have spread southward, invading the tropical hardwoods of Key Largo.

The thought of pythons, some reported to be over 10 feet long, slowed my movement through the forest. It had me looking up at the overhanging branches, as well as down at the coral boulders strewn along the path. I walked watchfully, spotting many small lizards that scurried away before my footsteps. But I saw no snakes that day.

There are many ecological reasons why a python should not be where I was hoping to see one. My conscience told me this. But the adventure lover in me thrilled to the possibility of yet another fascinating reptile in our midst.

AUTHOR'S NOTE

The question I am asked most often is, "Are you afraid of snakes?" The answer is yes. I'm a little afraid of all reptiles, but not so afraid that I cannot appreciate their beauty and enjoy watching them.

All reptiles will bite if cornered or threatened. To defend themselves, snakes can do little more than bite. Lizards and turtles not only bite—they can scratch with their sharp toenails. And any bite or scratch from a wild animal can be serious. I do carry a snake-bite kit and know how to use it. But in the event of a bite from a venomous snake, my plan is to get to a hospital as quickly as possible. I try not to get

close enough to be bitten. All of my up-close reptile watching is done with binoculars or telephoto camera lenses.

The majority of reptiles in this section were painted from photos or video footage I've taken in wild places all across the country. A number of the rare or exotic reptiles were photographed in zoos or private collections.

My wife, Deanna, and I have searched for reptiles from New England to the Sonoran Desert to the Grand Canyon. We have found them across the Great Plains, the middle South, and in the deep South. Our favorite places to photograph reptiles are in the bayous of Louisiana, Georgia's Okeefenokee Swamp, South Carolina's Four Holes Swamp, and the Florida Everglades. I encourage you to include these amazing locations on your lifetime list of places to see for yourself.

GOLDEN EAGLE

Thunder Birds

NATURE'S FLYING PREDATORS

Recently I set out with my wife, Deanna, who is my partner in adventure, to revisit many of our favorite places to find birds. Only *this* time around we were seeking only the largest and most powerful birds. We found many, from great tom turkeys to huge sandhill cranes that stood five feet tall. But the big birds I wanted to paint were the birds that hunted prey or caught fish—nature's flying predators.

I named my awesome subjects after the Thunderbird, a giant eagle-like Native American spirit that brought the thunder and lightning. My Thunder Birds are the biggest and strongest of birds that, with piercing talon or stabbing bill, reign fiercely over smaller wildlife. These birds make it easy to believe that dinosaurs never really died off, but are living today in the form of eagles, hawks, vultures, owls, herons, and pelicans.

Besides traveling to the wild places where we knew these birds would be, we also visited sanctuaries where wounded birds are being kept and cared for. Wherever birds were, we went to see them. Whenever we had a chance to learn more about them, we took advantage of it.

Marvel at these awe-inspiring creatures with us. I've painted many of them life-size and have made all of them as realistic as I possibly could so you will see the same light Deanna and I saw in their wild eyes.

67

BALD EAGLE

Eagles, Hawks, and Falcons

I once helped a biologist friend repair the wing of a wounded wild eagle. I held the eagle firmly by the feet as my friend sewed the damaged wing muscle. As I held the big bird's ankles together, the eagle bent its body toward my hands and probed at my skin with its large, curved beak, gently touching my knuckles and fingers. At first I was alarmed but my friend explained that an eagle uses its beak primarily to eat and to preen its feathers, not to defend itself. As long as I held the bird's powerful feet, preventing them from striking out and slashing us with their sharp talons (claws), we were safe.

Eagles, hawks, and falcons combine flight speed with strong grasping feet to subdue and kill a wide variety of small animals. They strike quickly from the sky, literally bowling their victims over by crashing into them and knocking them down.

Watching one of these big and powerful birds of prey catch and kill its food is one of the most spectacular and shocking sights you can witness in nature. Seeing it all up close through binoculars or through a telephoto camera lens can raise the hair on the back of your neck.

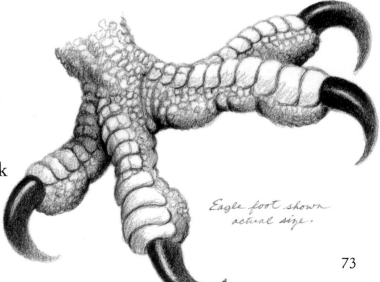

Eagle foot shown actual size.

SNOWY OWL

Owls

We can only imagine the terror a mouse or rabbit experiences when fleeing an eagle or a hawk attack, as it is quickly overcome by the sound and fury of wing beats. In sharp contrast, animals killed by owls are taken unaware, never knowing what hit them.

An owl's wing feathers are soft and are separated at the tips to sift air rather than slice through it. This makes owl wings silent in flight. An owl's feathered feet also have soft edges for silent flight. Prey animals are taken suddenly and without warning in the midst of whatever they happen to be doing. Only in bright moonlight might an owl's intended victim sense what is coming, when it sees the hunter's large shadow moving across the ground.

At night in the forest, while I was taking flash photos of owls, one of the big birds swooped down toward me from behind, lightly brushing my head with its wings. I felt it and then I saw it, but I never heard it coming.

Owl wing feathers

An owl's feathered foot

77

BLACK VULTURES

Vultures

Vultures do not usually kill to eat. They feed on carrion—animals they find that are already dead. In North America there is the turkey vulture, named for its red, turkey-like head, and the black vulture, whose head is gray.

Vultures find food visually or by smell. The odor of carrion rises in columns of warm air called thermals. Vultures soar high, kept aloft by these same thermals, and circle in the sky until they smell the scent or see carrion to eat.

When a vulture finds food, it must eat it wherever it may be. Vulture feet are not strong enough to lift and move things. This is why we see vultures feeding on roadkill right on the road, flying off and returning to their food each time a vehicle passes. To eat, a vulture uses its sharp beak to rip open holes in a dead animal's skin. Then it pokes its head inside to tear away bits of flesh. Vultures have naked heads, which are cleaner than feathers for feeding inside an animal carcass. The vulture's head at the far left is shown life-size.

In the Everglades, Deanna and I saw a flock of black vultures feeding on an old alligator that had died. The big birds tore holes in the soft skin on the alligator's belly and fed on the flesh inside. In less than a week, they had reduced the eight-foot alligator to a floating skin bag of bones.

drying after a shower

Black Vulture

Turkey Vulture

Identifying vultures by shape and pattern:

BLACK VULTURE
Length: 25 inches
Wingspan: 56 inches

TURKEY VULTURE
Length: 27 inches
Wingspan: 70 inches

GREAT BLUE HERON AND BROWN WATER SNAKE

Herons and Egrets

Of all the birds that I watch, I love watching herons and egrets the most. There is such suspense in the way they slowly stalk fish in shallow water, bill downward, long neck poised to strike. The eyes of herons and egrets are set in such a way that they can look downward to watch for prey or forward to give the birds binocular vision and the depth perception necessary to spear a moving target in the water. Herons and egrets will wade in water as deep as their legs are long, but never so deep that they wet their feathers or lose their footing on the bottom. Afloat, they are easy prey for big snapping turtles or alligators.

The largest of these birds is the great blue heron, standing over 40 inches tall. A great blue heron can catch and swallow a fish its own weight or a snake as long as the heron is tall.

Deanna spotted a great blue heron with a water snake that hung down to the heron's feet. A snake that size would have had to be killed by heavy blows and chops to the head from the heron's big spear-shaped beak. The lifeless snake was swallowed whole, headfirst, a little at a time, until it was all down.

forward-facing eyes

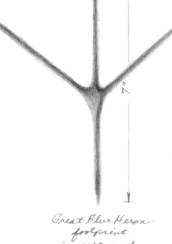

Great Blue Heron footprint in soft mud.

You can recognize a flying heron or egret by its long bill and long legs.

BROWN PELICAN

Pelicans

We were sitting in the shade of a rustic little hut on the edge of a fishing wharf when the sky suddenly clouded over and it began to rain, then pour. The heavy drops made loud popping sounds as they hit the tin roof of our shelter. Outside in the rain a brown pelican perched on a dock piling and began swaying rhythmically forward and backward, side to side, with its head facing upward and bill wide open. The pelican was catching raindrops to quench its thirst! Suddenly, I wanted to go out in the downpour and drink rainwater, too.

A brown pelican (50 inches long, with a wingspan of 80 inches) is the kind of bird that makes you wonder what it would be like to live outdoors in the sun and wind, weathering every storm. What is it like to go flying over the ocean waves and diving for your supper?

When a brown pelican sees a fish in the water, it simply drops down headfirst to catch it. As soon as the pelican hits the surface it opens its bill, filling its throat pouch with water, which widens its mouth in order to trap its catch.

Brown pelicans are coastal dwellers. American white pelicans can be found on seacoasts and also inland on large freshwater lakes, marshes, and rivers. American white pelicans are not divers. They catch fish as a flock by swimming close together and driving whole schools of frantic fish into shallow water where they can be scooped up one or two at a time into the pelicans' bills.

Pelicans have the largest bills of all birds. The top bill is made of highly porous bone; it weighs only three or four ounces. The bottom bill is pliable and opens wide to engulf fish. The throat pouch is made of flexible, stretchable skin.

Catching raindrops.

Diving for a fish.

Throat pouch expanding.

White Pelicans fishing together.

COMMON LOON
(life-size)
Length: 34 inches
Wingspan: 58 inches

DOUBLE-CRESTED CORMORANT
Length: 33 inches
Wingspan: 50 inches

GREAT CORMORANT
Length: 36 inches
Wingspan: 60 inches

NORTHERN GANNET
(life-size)
Length: 36 inches
Wingspan: 72 inches

Loons, Cormorants, and Gannets

Pelicans dive just under the water surface for fish. They are not deep divers. The deep-diving birds are the loons, cormorants, and gannets. Gannets are strictly saltwater birds. Loons and cormorants are found in saltwater and in freshwater.

The loon is the deep-diving champ, swimming down 200 feet or more to catch swift fish, which are stabbed, speared, or grasped in the loon's sturdy pointed bill. You can get a sense of just how far and fast a loon can swim underwater by noting the time and place that the bird submerges and the time and place that it resurfaces.

Loons have a weirdly human-sounding call: *WaahooohAAA!* They are heavy birds that require a long flyway to become airborne, so loons will only land on bodies of water large enough to allow them to take off again.

Cormorants do not dive as deep as loons, but they dive deep enough to catch bottom-feeding fish and crustaceans. Neither loons nor cormorants plunge from the air to dive in water. They dive from a floating position and power underwater, propelled by their large webbed feet. A cormorant will often "snorkel" with body afloat and head poked underwater to look around before diving.

Gannets are almost as large as pelicans, but are more streamlined and are much more spectacular divers. Gannets dive from heights of 150 feet, and they hit the water with a tremendous splash. You can identify a gannet simply by the height of its dive and the size of its splash. They dive down as deep as 40 feet and swim into schools of herring, slashing and cutting the fish with their sharp bills.

Loon diving.

Cormorant snorkeling.

All diving birds have strong, short legs set far back on the body and large webbed feet.

91

OSPREY WITH TROUT

Nature's Flying Predators

I love being out in open country and seeing an eagle or a hawk wheeling slowly overhead. And when one alights on a tree, I run to get a closer look. If I'm lucky, the bird will stay awhile and I'll see it ruffle the feathers on its back or spread its wings for a few audible flaps. I wonder about everything birds do, and I want you to wonder, too.

The next time you watch an osprey carrying a freshly caught fish, try to imagine the bird's actual size. How big and heavy would it be if it perched on your outstretched arm? How wide would its wings spread? How long and curved and sharp are its talons? And how many fish must it catch to feed itself and its family back in the nest?

Birds know a freedom of movement and space that we can only imagine. They have a limitless sky in which to fly and the whole world to come down to. Up high, they can see the patchwork of the landscape, the expanse of the sea, and the broad curve of the horizon. They climb on air and ride the wind. They hover, flap, glide, and soar. Everything about them is fascinating. And the big predatory birds fascinate us the most. Nature's flying predators are magnificent creatures of the earth and water as well as of the sky.

AUTHOR'S NOTE

The life-size paintings in this section, done in acrylic paint and white chalk pencil, are the result of many years of research in the field and thousands of miles of travel. Here are some of the places Deanna and I have visited again and again in our search for America's birds.

Attwater Prairie Chicken NWR*, TX
Bear River NWR, UT
Bombay Hook NWR, DE
Chincoteague NWR, VA
Crocodile Lake NWR, FL
Custer State Park, SD
Dead Creek Wildlife Management Area, VT
Everglades National Park, FL
Four Holes Swamp Audubon Sanctuary, SC
Great Dismal Swamp NWR, VA
Hawk Mountain Sanctuary, PA
Iroquois NWR, NY
J.N. "Ding" Darling NWR, FL
Loxahatchee NWR, FL
Merritt Island NWR, FL
Middle Creek Wildlife Area, PA
Missisquoi NWR, VT

Mississippi Sandhill Crane NWR, MS
Montezuma NWR, NY
Okefenokee NWR, GA
Sabine NWR, LA
Salt Plains NWR, OK
Saguaro National Park, AZ
St. Augustine Alligator Farm and Zoological Park, FL
San Pedro River Riparian National Conservation Area, AZ
Savannah NWR, SC
Tallgrass Prairie Preserve, OK
Tonto National Forest, AZ
Vermont Institute of Natural Science, VT
Yellowstone National Park, WY

*NWR stands for "National Wildlife Refuge"

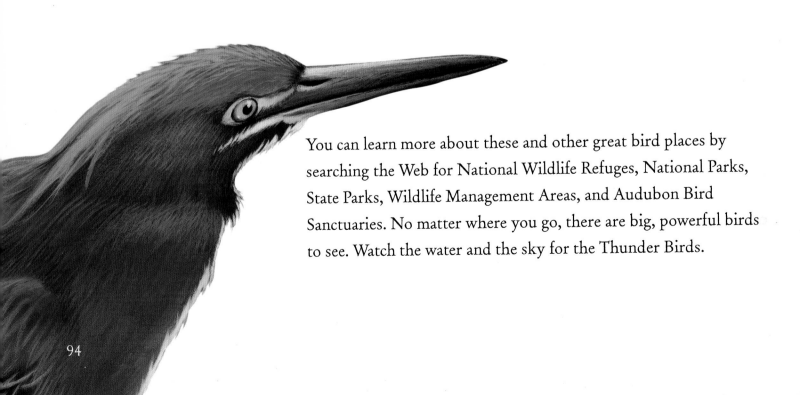

You can learn more about these and other great bird places by searching the Web for National Wildlife Refuges, National Parks, State Parks, Wildlife Management Areas, and Audubon Bird Sanctuaries. No matter where you go, there are big, powerful birds to see. Watch the water and the sky for the Thunder Birds.